PIANO · VOCAL · GUITAR

CHART HITS OF
2014-2015

ISBN 978-1-4950-1229-7

HAL•LEONARD®
CORPORATION
7777 W. BLUEMOUND RD. P.O. BOX 13819 MILWAUKEE, WI 53213

Visit Hal Leonard Online at
www.halleonard.com

ALL ABOUT THAT BASS

Words and Music by KEVIN KADISH
and MEGHAN TRAINOR

Be-cause you know I'm all a-bout that bass, 'bout that bass. No tre - ble. I'm all a-bout that bass, 'bout that bass. No tre - ble. I'm all a-bout that bass, 'bout that bass. No tre - ble. I'm all a-bout that bass, 'bout that bass, bass, bass, bass, bass.

E7

Nah, ___ I'm just playin'. I know you think you're fat. ___

D.S. al Coda

But I'm here to tell ya ev-'ry

CODA

bass. Be-cause you know I'm

Bm

all a-bout that bass, 'bout that bass. No tre-ble. I'm all a-bout that bass, 'bout that

E7

bass. No tre-ble. I'm all a-bout that bass, 'bout that

bass. No tre - ble. I'm all a - bout that bass, 'bout that bass. Be-cause you know I'm

bass.

ANIMALS

Words and Music by ADAM LEVINE,
BEN LEVIN and SHELLBACK

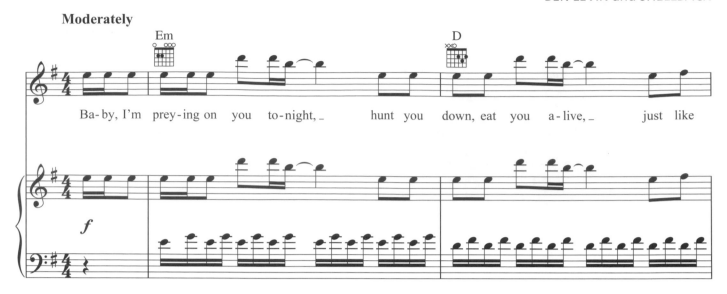

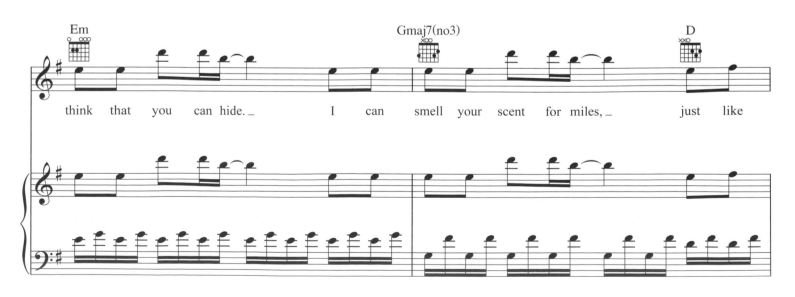

BANG BANG

Words and Music by ONIKA MARAJ,
MAX MARTIN, SAVAN KOTECHA
and RICKARD GÖRANSSON

With a groove

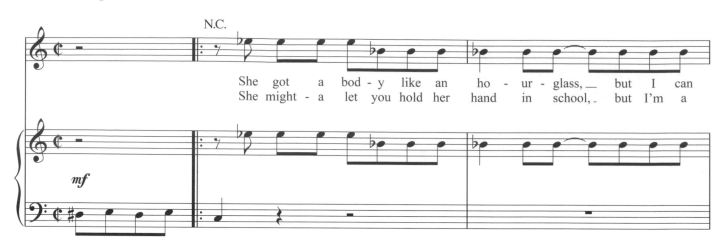

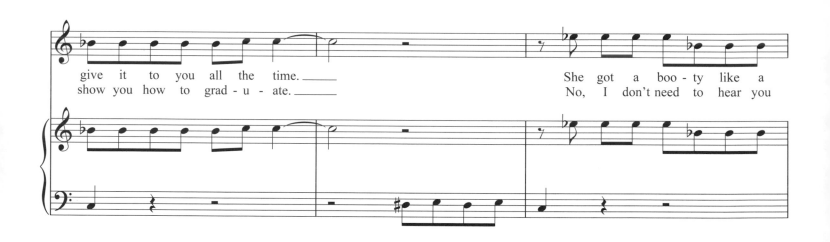

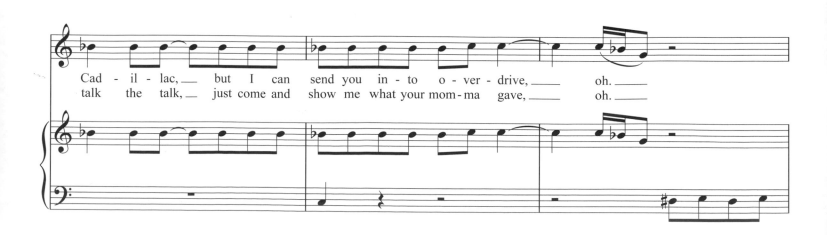

BLAME

Words and Music by CALVIN HARRIS,
JOHN NEWMAN and JAMES NEWMAN

COOL KIDS

Words and Music by GRAHAM SIEROTA,
JAMIE SIEROTA, NOAH SIEROTA,
SYDNEY SIEROTA, JEFFREY DAVID SIEROTA
and JESIAH DZWONEK

'cause all the cool kids, they seem to { fit in. / get it. } I wish that I could

be like the cool kids, like the cool kids. _____

Repeat and Fade

Optional Ending

DON'T

Words and Music by ED SHEERAN,
DAWN ROBINSON, BEN LEVIN,
RAPHAEL SAADIQ, ALI JONES-MUHAMMAD
and CONESHA OWENS

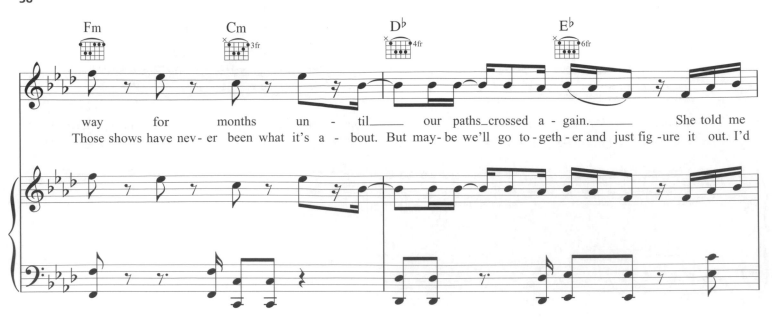

way   for   months   un - til____   our paths crossed a - gain._____   She told me
Those shows have nev - er been what it's a - bout. But may - be we'll go to - geth - er and just fig - ure it out. I'd

I   was   nev - er   look - ing   for   a   friend.   May - be   you   can
ra - ther   put   on a   film   with   you   and   sit   on the   couch.   But   we   should

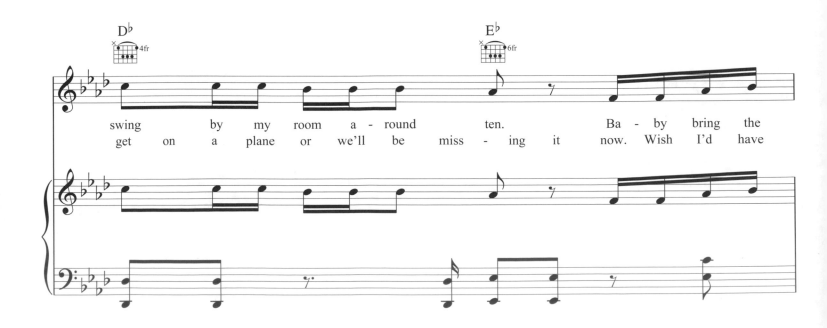

swing   by   my   room a - round   ten.   Ba - by   bring   the
get   on   a   plane   or   we'll   be   miss - ing   it   now.   Wish   I'd   have

42

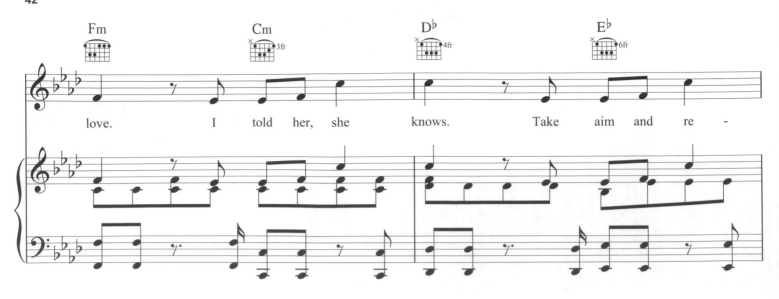

Verse 3:

[Knock, knock, knock] on my hotel door.
I don't even know if she knows what for.
She was crying on my shoulder.
I already told ya.
Trust and respect is what we do this for.
I never intended to be next.
But you didn't need to take him to bed, that's all.
And I never saw him as a threat.
Until you disappeared with him to have sex, of course.
It's not like we were both on tour.
We were staying on the same ****ing hotel floor.
And I wasn't looking for a promise to commitment.
But it was never just fun and I thought you were different.
This is not the way you realise what you wanted.
It's a bit too much too late if I'm honest.
All this time, god knows, I'm singin':

HABITS
(Stay High)

Words and Music by TOVE LO,
JAKOB JERLSTRÖM and LUDVIG SÖDERBERG

Moderate Pop beat

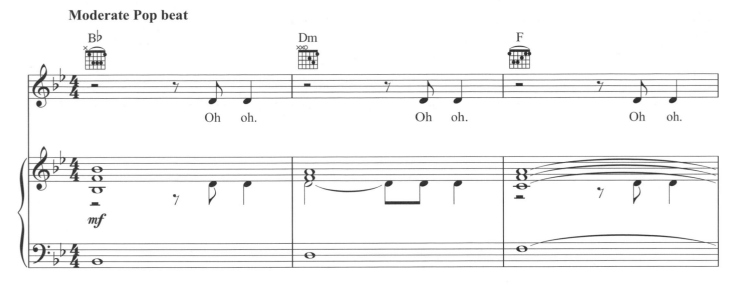

Oh oh.   Oh oh.   Oh oh.

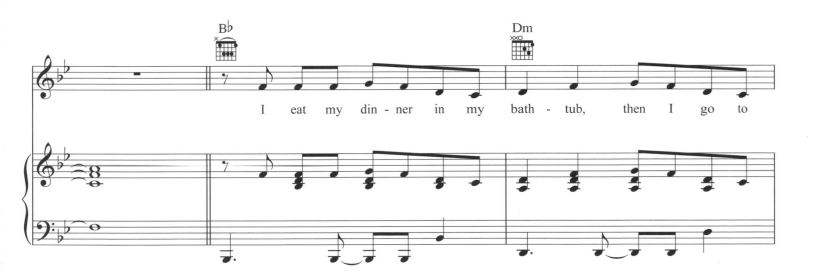

I eat my din-ner in my bath-tub, then I go to

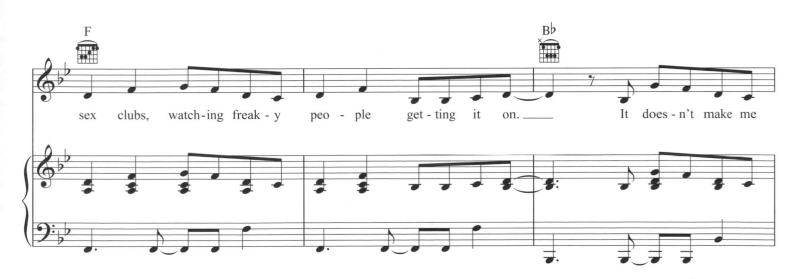

sex clubs, watch-ing freak-y peo-ple get-ting it on. ___ It does-n't make me

I'M NOT THE ONLY ONE

Words and Music by SAM SMITH
and JAMES NAPIER

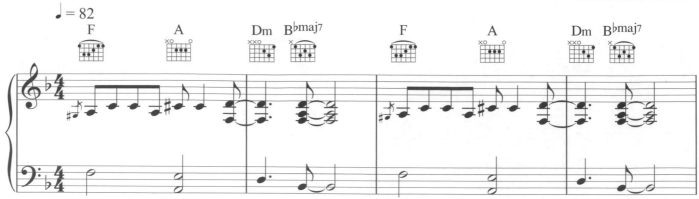

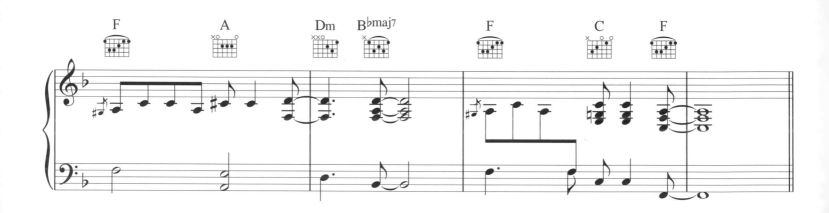

1. You and me, we made a vow for bet-ter or for worse.

RIPTIDE

Words and Music by
VANCE JOY

Recorded a half step higher.

RUDE

Words and Music by NASRI ATWEH,
MARK PELLIZZER, ALEX TANAS,
BEN SPIVAK and ADAM MESSINGER

Moderate Reggae

* *Recorded a half step higher.*

SHAKE IT OFF

Words and Music by TAYLOR SWIFT,
MAX MARTIN and SHELLBACK

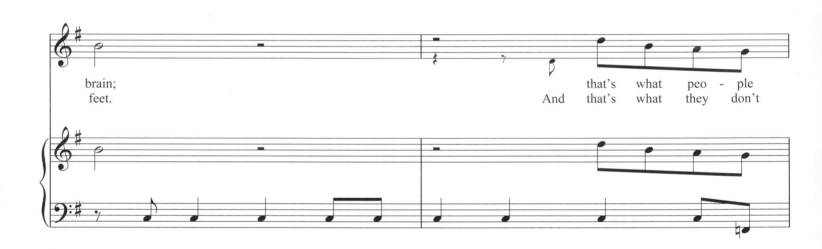

mm. I go on too man - y dates,
mm. I'm danc - ing on my own;

but I can't make 'em stay;
I make the moves up as I go.

at least, that's what peo - ple say, _____ mm,
And that's what they don't know, _____ mm,

mm. That's what peo - ple say, _____ mm,
mm. That's what they don't know, _____ mm,

70

Additional Lyrics

Spoken: *Hey, hey, hey! Just think: While you've been getting*
Down and out about the liars and the dirty, dirty
Cheats of the world, you could've been getting down to
This. Sick. Beat!

Rap: My ex-man brought his new girlfriend.
She's like, "Oh, my god!" But I'm just gonna shake.
And to the fella over there with the hella good hair,
Won't you come on over, baby? We can shake, shake, shake.

A SKY FULL OF STARS

Words and Music by GUY BERRYMAN,
JON BUCKLAND, WILL CHAMPION,
CHRIS MARTIN and TIM BERGLING

Moderate Dance groove

Lyrics:

'Cause you're a sky, _____ 'cause you're a
'Cause you're a sky, _____ 'cause you're a

sky _____ full of stars. _____ I'm gon - na
sky _____ full of stars. _____ I wan - na

give _____ you my heart. _____
die _____ in your arms. _____

*Recorded a half step higher.

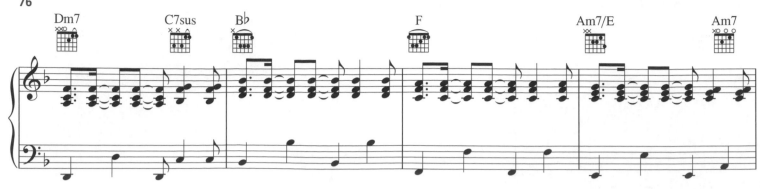

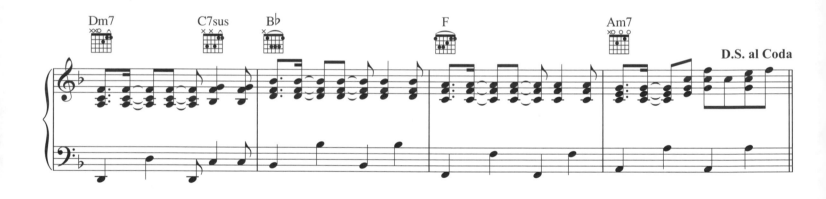

I think I see you. _____

'Cause you're a sky, ____ you're a sky _____ full of stars, ____

____ such a heav-en-ly view. _____

You're such a heav-en-ly view.

STEAL MY GIRL

Words and Music by LOUIS TOMLINSON,
LIAM PAYNE, JULIAN BUNETTA,
WAYNE HECTOR, EDWARD DREWETT
and JOHN RYAN

Moderate Rock beat

SUPERHEROES

Words and Music by DANIEL O'DONOGHUE,
MARK SHEEHAN and JAMES BARRY

YELLOW FLICKER BEAT

from THE HUNGER GAMES: MOCKINGJAY PART 1

Words and Music by ELLA YELICH O'CONNOR
and JOEL LITTLE

Moderate Electro Pop

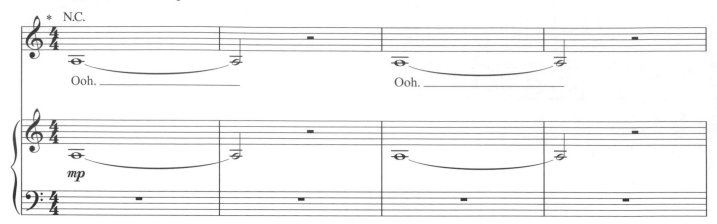

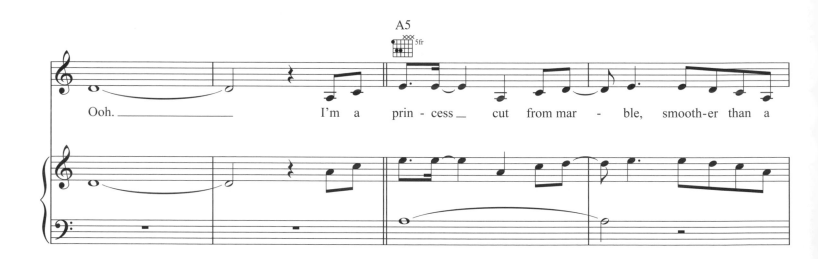

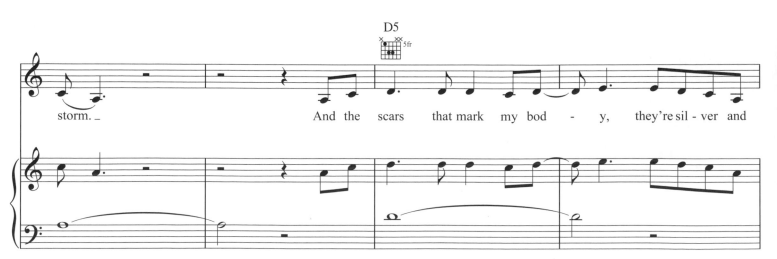

* Recorded a half step lower.

shiv - ers move down my shoul - der blades _ in dou - ble time.

Ooh, now peo - ple talk to me, I'm slip - ping out of reach, now.

Peo - ple talk to me and all their fac - es blur. _ But I got my fin - gers laced to - geth - er, and I

made a lit - tle pri - son and I'm lock - ing up ev - 'ry - one who ev - er laid a fin - ger on

TAKE ME TO CHURCH

Words and Music by
ANDREW HOZIER-BYRNE

Moderate Ballad

My lov-er's got hu-mour, she's the gig-gle at a fu-n'ral.

Knows ev-'ry-bod-y's dis-ap-prov-al, I should-'ve wor-shipped her soon-er.

If the heav-ens ev-er did speak, she's the last _ true mouth-piece. Ev-'ry Sun-day's get-ting more bleak,

To Coda

I'll tell you my sins __ and you can sharp-en your knife. __ Of-fer me __ that death-less death and, good God, __ __ let me give you my life. If I'm a pa-gan of the good times, my __ lov-er's the sun-light. To keep the god-dess on my __ side, she de-mands a sac-ri - fice. Drain the whole sea, get some-thing shin - y. Some-thing meat-y for the main course,